THE NOISE BENEATH MY SKIN

VOICING THE CHAOS OF INVISIBLE STRUGGLES WITHIN THE MIND

By

Kay Star

Printed in the United States of America.

First printing edition 2026.

Dedication

To every soul who carries unseen battles—

the restless, the weary, the quietly undone.

I am among you. I know the weight of a mind that falters,

the silence that lingers behind forced smiles.

And so I offer this truth, steady and certain:

You are not alone.

In the depths, where shadows feel endless,

there are others walking beside you—unseen, yet understanding.

If today you have only endured, let that be enough.

Even survival is a quiet, extraordinary act.

TABLE OF CONTENTS

Introduction 1

Part I: Losing Control 2

Addiction 3

Binge eating 8

Bulimia 12

Anorexia 15

Hoarding 17

Pica 20

Narcolepsy 23

Part II: Fractured Thinking 27

Delusional disorder 28

Cotard's Delusion 31

Confusion 35

Intrusive thoughts 38

Psychosis 41

Schizophrenia 45

Ekbom Syndrome 48

Part III: Memory & Identity 52

Alzheimer's 53

Amnesia 55

Dissociative identity disorder 58

Dissociating 61

Mutism 64

Psychogenic non-epileptic seizures 67

Part IV: Inner Battles 72

Depression 73

Intermittent Explosive Disorder 75

Bipolar 78
ADHD 82
Autism 85
OCD 91
Insomnia 93
Kufungisisa 96
Opposition defiance disorder 99
Panic disorder 102
Phobias 105
PTSD 110
Separation anxiety 114
Sleep paralysis 118
Tourette syndrome 121
Emotional regulation disorder 124

Part V: Self & Perception 128

Body dysmorphia disorder 129
Avoidant personality disorder 133
Antisocial Personality Disorder 137
Apotemnophilia 140
Excoriation disorder 143
Narcissistic personality disorder 146
Paranoid Personality Disorder 149
Dyslexia 152

Part VI: Belonging & Change 156

Culture shock 157

"Pause & Reflect" 161

In the end, take a moment. 162
Now write one sentence to yourself, not perfect, just honest. 163

INTRODUCTION

Kirsten is a courageous writer who uses her personal journey with mental health challenges to bring comfort, understanding, and hope to others. Through honesty and compassion, she shares a message for anyone facing difficult days that they are seen, valued, and never alone. Her writing is rooted in empathy and a desire to help readers feel supported, understood, and encouraged on their own path toward healing.

PART I: LOSING CONTROL

Addiction

It isn't just a thought—it's a need to know,
why he chose that path, why he let me go.
What does it give him I couldn't be?
What kind of pull steals him from me?
So I tell myself it's just one try,
just one breath to answer why.
It hits like fire beneath my skin,
a violent rush that drags me in.
My heart misfires, then starts to race,
like it's trying hard to leave this place.
My jaw locks tight, my hands won't rest,
a pounding echo in my chest.
The world turns sharp, too bright, too loud—
I feel untouchable, unbound—
and for one second, I can see
why I was never enough to be.
But one turns two, then three, then more,
until I'm someone I wasn't before—

a hollow shape inside my skin,
with something restless living in.
The nights stretch out, refuse to end,
I lose the line of foe and friend.
My body aches for sleep, for air,
but I ignore it like it isn't there.
It's not a choice, it's not a fight—
it's just surviving one more night.
My mind unravels thread by thread,
something splintering in my head.
Thoughts don't land—they crash and spin,
then turn against me from within.
Voices twist the things I hear,
make every silence feel severe.
Shadows breathe and start to stay,
they follow me into the day.
Every glance feels sharp, untrue,
like something's watching what I do.
I try to hold on, but slip away—
I can't tell night from broken day.
Everything I love slips through my hands,

like I'm made of dust, like nothing stands.
Names fade out, faces blur,
I don't know them—I don't know her.
The sound of laughter feels too far,
like it belongs to who we were.
No place feels safe, no voice feels mine,
I disappear a piece at a time.
What's left of me begins to cave,
a body worn I couldn't save.
My reflection won't meet my eyes,
just something hollow in disguise.
No voice, no place, no memory—
just something this has turned me to be.
I reach for something I can't replace,
dig through the dark, through empty space.
But every part I try to find
is buried somewhere in my mind.
And in the end, there's almost nothing,
just a pulse that keeps on stuttering.
A slowing breath, a fading ache,
a body I no longer wake.

No grand goodbye, no final plea—

just silence closing in on me.

No one hears, no one remains—

what's left of me

just fades away.

BUT MAYBE...

in the dark, something resists—
a quiet voice that still exists.
It calls me back, it says my name,

reminds me I am not this pain.
So I gather shards I thought were gone,
hold them close, keep moving on.

Not fixed, not whole—but still I stand,
with trembling heart and open hand.

Binge eating

The daylight fades, the room is still,

A sudden urge I cannot kill.

It isn't food the body seeks,

But something in the silence speaks—

A yawning void inside the chest,

A weary soul that pleads for rest.

The pantry opens, reason slips,

As sugar passes through the lips.

The fingers grasp, the jaw works fast,

A desperate hope the numb will last.

The sweet and salty, soft and dry,

Consumed to drown an inner cry.

The wrappers tear, the cartons fall,

A driven need to eat it all.

No time to plate, no time to sit,

Just swallowing the weight of it.

A dizzy blur, a fevered pace,

To fill the dark and empty space.

The chewing turns mechanical,

The urge feels uncontrollable.

Until the stomach starts to ache,

From every rapid bite I take.

A frantic race that can't be won,

Until the heavy task is done.

And then the silence rushes back,

A suffocating, heavy black.

The spell is broken, truth returns,

And deep inside, the body burns.

Not just with fullness, but with shame,

The cruel, familiar, quiet blame.

"I'll start tomorrow," whispers fear,

A hollow vow I barely hear.

The secret cycle spins around,

Where grip is lost and guilt is found.

A silent battle fought alone,

Behind closed doors, to most unknown.

But this is not a lack of will,

Nor just an emptiness to fill.

It is a heavy, tangled chain,

A mind attempting to soothe its pain.

There's grace within the steps to heal,

To learn to breathe, and simply feel.

BUT MAYBE...

I will pause, not fight, not flee,
just sit a moment, breathe, and see.
What feeling waits beneath the need?

What truth is asking to be freed?
And if I fall, I'll meet that place
with steady eyes and gentle grace.

For healing grows when shame is gone,
and every breath can lead me on.

Bulimia

It starts like a spark you can't ignore,
a pull that drags you to the door,
just one bite—then something slips,
and silence breaks between your lips.
Too fast to taste, too full to feel,
a spinning, breathless kind of real,
like filling up a bottomless space
that never keeps what you embrace.
Your hands don't pause, your mind goes dim,
the edges blur, the light grows thin,
and somewhere deep a voice goes quiet
while something louder starts a riot.
Then suddenly—it all comes back,
a crashing wave, a sharp attack,
the fullness heavy, thick, and wrong,
like you've been holding it too long.
And shame steps in before you breathe,
it tangles tight, it will not leave,

it tells you fix it, make it right,
erase yourself before the light.
So back you go, not out of peace,
not even hope for real release,
just chasing some imagined line
where "less" will finally feel like "fine."
But every loop just pulls you through
the same old ache, the same untrue—
that you are better, smaller, gone,
when all along you've still been one.
There is no "enough" in that demand,
no steady ground, no place to stand,
just more and less in endless swing—
until you question everything.
But even here, where it feels stuck,
where every turn feels out of luck,
there's still a part that hasn't caved—
the one that knows you can be saved.

BUT MAYBE...

I must pause before the tide,
and sit with what I try to hide.
A breath, a beat, a moment's grace,

to meet myself in softer space.
And if I slip, I will not fall
beyond the reach of care at all.

For healing isn't straight or fast—
it's choosing kindness that can last.

Anorexia

The silence in the kitchen is a heavy, grey shroud,
The hunger is a whisper that's becoming too loud.
It's a hollowed-out feeling, a cave in the chest,
Where the ghost of a person is trying to rest.
The numbers are masters, the scale is a god,
And the path that I'm walking is lonely and odd.
I am fading in pieces, I am losing the light,
To fit in a shadow that's ever too tight.
There's a coldness that settles deep under the skin,
A debt that is paid for the "crime" of being thin.
The eyes become sunken, the spirit grows frayed,
By the debt of a body that's being unpaid.
It's a quiet disappearing, a slow, steady grief,
Where the smaller I get, the less there is relief.
Just a cage made of ivory, a heart out of breath,
In a race where the finish line feels like a death.

BUT MAYBE...

Recovery isn't a straight, shining line,
It's a jagged ascent through the thicket and vine.
It's choosing the salt, the fat, and the flame,

And learning to love the weight of your name.
I will not flinch at the tears or the rage,
As you break the gold bars of your self-chosen cage.

We'll nourish the garden, the muscle, the mind,
Leaving the "perfect" and "empty" behind.
Eat for the morning. Eat for the grace.

Eat to take up your rightful space.
The world is too wide for a life lived in small;
I am right here to catch you. I won't let you fall

Hoarding

It didn't begin like this at all,
no towering stacks, no crowded hall—
just quiet keeping, small and slight,
to hold what slipped away from sight.
A broken mug, a shirt, a note,
a thousand things you couldn't tote
into the past where they belong,
so you kept them, holding on.
Each object hummed: remember me,
don't let me fade, don't set me free—
as if by saving every part
you could outpace a breaking heart.
The floor grew smaller, inch by inch,
the walls crept close, the air would pinch,
you turned sideways to exist,
inside a life you somehow missed.
"I'll clean tomorrow," soft you say,
but fear keeps pulling you away—

because to choose what goes or stays
means facing loss in countless ways.
And oh, it aches to finally see
the weight of all this memory—
the things you kept to make you whole
have slowly swallowed up your soul.
Not loud, not sharp, but deep and slow,
a quiet, constant undertow—
where every item feels like proof
you've loved, you've lost, you've held the truth.
So still you keep, you cannot sever,
each piece feels tied to every ever—
and buried there, beneath the weight,
you sit, and hope it's not too late.

BUT MAYBE...

I am more than what I store,
not every thing must fill my floor.
The past still lives without each piece,

and letting go can bring me peace.
So I will start with just one part,
a single step, a steady heart.

One choice, one space, one breath made clear—
I keep what serves, release what's fear.
And if it's hard, I'll still be kind,

this change takes time, I'll move in time.
For space can hold both loss and grace—
and I deserve a gentler place.

Pica

It isn't hunger, not quite the same,

but something restless without a name.

A quiet itch beneath the skin,

a pull toward what I shouldn't begin.

The paper bends, a fragile tear,

a brittle sound I strain to hear.

I fold the edge, I taste the dry,

and wonder softly—why am I?

Chalk like dust upon my tongue,

a hollow song that's never sung.

It breaks to nothing, fades too fast,

yet leaves a ghost I try to grasp.

The soil calls with iron breath,

a scent of rain, of life, of death.

I hold it close, then hesitate—

is this a need, or just a weight?

Soap like silk, so smooth, so wrong,

a fleeting urge that won't stay long.

It glides, it gleams, a quiet dare,
a clean that isn't meant to share.
This isn't taste that draws me near,
but texture whispered in my ear.
A rhythm strange, a subtle bluff,
a craving built on not enough.
Yet in the pause, I start to see
the line between the urge and me.
And though it calls, I let it pass—
a fleeting shadow, not to last

BUT MAYBE...

I am not this urge alone,
it's just a signal I've been shown.
A need for comfort, sense, or ground,

that's asking softly to be found.
So I will pause before I choose,
and give my body safer use.

Find other ways my hands can cope,
with steady care and gentle hope.
And step by step, I'll learn to see

what helps, what heals, what's good for me.

Narcolepsy

I fall asleep in half-spoke lines,

Between the pauses, commas, signs,

A sentence breaking into air—

I'm gone before it's fully there.

Mid-laughter, while the moment gleams,

I'm stolen softly into dreams,

The world still spinning, bright and loud,

While I slip silent through the crowd.

A fork held still, a ringing phone,

A voice that suddenly's alone,

The smallest pause, the slightest seam—

And I am pulled into a dream.

No warning bell, no gentle fade,

No careful choice or bargain made,

Just gravity I cannot fight

That drags me under out of sight.

Conversations blur and bend,

I lose the middle and the end,

Faces flicker, then they're gone—

But time for everyone moves on.

I wake to fragments, out of place,

A different look on every face,

A question hanging in the air—

They don't quite know I wasn't there.

And so I live in broken streams,

Half in the world and half in dreams,

Forever falling, it would seem,

Between each moment—lost in between

BUT MAYBE...

this is not a lack of will,
nor proof that I am weak or still.
My body moves by different cues,

a rhythm I can learn to use.
So I will plan with care and grace,
make room for rest, a steady pace.

Short pauses built into my day
can help me find a safer way.
And I am more than when I sleep,

more than the hours I can keep.
For even drifting, soft or deep,
my worth is mine alone to keep.

Even in loss of control, there is still a quiet part of you trying to find its way back.

PART II: FRACTURED THINKING

Delusional disorder

The world you walk is anchored fast to things that you can touch,
But I have found a different weight that matters twice as much.
It started as a single thread, a stray and silver line,
That wove itself through everything and whispered, "This is mine."
I see the way the traffic lights are blinking out a code,
A map for me to follow down a long and private road;
To you, the stranger's glancing eye is nothing but a blur,
To me, it is the witness to the things that must occur.
I build a cathedral out of hints and bricks of "maybe so,"
Until the "maybe" turns to "yes," the only truth I know.
There is a logic in the tilt, a reason in the sway,
A grand design that hides behind the clutter of the day.
You bring me facts like heavy stones to break my windows in,
But facts are merely paper shields against the life I spin;
The more you try to show me where the seams of truth are frayed,
The more I see the clever way the trap was truly laid.
It is a quiet, glass-walled room where I am kept alone,
A kingdom made of iron thoughts upon a velvet throne.

I am the hero of a play that only I can see,

Or else the target of a plot that's focused just on me.

It isn't madness—not the kind that screams or sees the ghost—

It's the certainty of knowing what the world denies the most.

It is the anchor in the storm, the compass in the dark,

A fire fueled by evidence from every passing spark.

You call it a "disorder," or a fracture in the lens,

A bridge that starts in nowhere and in nowhere finally ends.

But how can I abandon what has given me the keys

To understand the heartbeat of the hidden conspiracies?

The mailbox isn't empty, and the sky is never blue

Without a secret meaning that was meant for me, not you.

I've stitched the sky to fit the earth, I've made the stars align,

To prove that while your world is real, this universe is mine.

I live within the fortress that my own conviction made,

A master of the mysteries, and never once afraid—

Except for when the silence grows and I am left to wonder

If the floor is solid ground, or if I'm falling under.

But then I see a pattern in the way the shadows fall,

And I am safe and certain, and I understand it all

BUT MAYBE…

feelings strong don't make it fact,
and minds can weave what's hard to track.
A thought can shout, insist, repeat,

yet still not stand on steady feet.
So I will pause and gently test
what feels so certain in my chest.

Seek other views, let voices in,
allow some doubt to slowly begin.
And I am more than what I think,

not every fear is a missing link.
With time, with help, with steady ground,
a clearer sense can still be found.

I don't walk this path alone,
there's strength in reaching, being known.

Cotard's Delusion

I know the date they say I breathe,

But I remember when I ceased—

A quiet slipping, thin and deep,

The kind of end that isn't sleep.

My heart performs a hollow drum,

A practiced lie it's become—

Each beat a sound without a cause,

A puppet bound by unseen laws.

They point—“You move, you speak, you see,”

But none of that belongs to me;

A body mimics what I was,

An echo shaped in human cause.

I've checked for warmth—there's nothing there,

No living spark beneath the air;

My hands feel carved from wax and doubt,

Preserved, but somehow hollowed out.

I walk through rooms like borrowed air,

No weight of soul, no presence there;

If I am here, then prove it true—

Why does the world pass through me too?

They fear my words, they call it wrong,

Say death's a place I don't belong—

But I have crossed, I know I did,

Somewhere between the breath I hid.

So let them speak of life and light,

I know my truth beyond their sight—

A quiet fact I cannot shed:

I am not living. I am dead

BUT MAYBE…

even now, I breathe, I feel,
the rise and fall, the steady real.
A pulse beneath, a subtle sign,

this body still is here, is mine.
These thoughts may come, they may repeat,
but they are not my living beat.

They pass like clouds across the sky,
not proof that I have ceased to be alive.
So I will ground in what is true—

the air I take, the sky I view.
A hand, a sound, a voice, a name,
small threads that tie me back again.

And if the doubt still lingers near,

I'll meet it soft, not ruled by fear.

For even lost, I still belong—

a quiet life, a steady song.

Confusion

The map's a blur I can't make clear,
The ink runs wild, the lines disappear.
The rain keeps falling, cold and slow,
I lose the path I used to know.
My words come out all twisted, wrong,
They falter weak instead of strong.
Where light once lived, now shadows creep,
And hums rise low where silence sleeps.
I walked this street not long ago,
Each turn was one I used to know.
But now the corners bend and slide,
Hollow turns with none to guide.
A fog rolls thick inside my head,
With static noise and threads that shred.
My focus slips, it won't remain,
Like grains of sand I cannot chain.
One truth becomes a fractured view,
It splits apart and doubles too.

Like mirrors facing into space,

Endless echoes I can't place.

So where to start, what thread to spin,

When every path just folds within?

The silence hums, it pulls me thin—

I stand here lost… where to begin

BUT MAYBE...

I think I might search for answers, sharp and true,
but find a thousand shifting views.
The more I chase, the less I see,

as doubt keeps circling back to me.
But maybe clarity's not loud,
not something rushing through a crowd.

Perhaps it comes in quiet space,
in slowing down, in giving grace.
So I will pause, release the race,

let stillness find a gentle place.
One step, one breath, one thought made clear—
the path will form from right here

Intrusive thoughts

There is a stranger living in the attic of my skull,

Rummaging through boxes, making the vibrant dull.

They speak in a dialect I never learned to use,

Bringing me headlines of terrible, fabricated news.

I didn't invite them, I didn't open the gate,

Yet they sit at my table and pile up the plate

With "maybe" and "must be" and "look what you've done,"

Blocking the warmth of my own internal sun.

A frequency tuned to a station of dread

A voice that sounds like me, but isn't what I said

A vision of a cliff when I'm standing on the floor.

It feels like a counterfeit, a forged signature on the soul,

A jagged little fragment trying to play the whole.

It says, "I am your secret," it says, "I am your core,"

But I've never seen this traveler's face before.

The trick is the distance—the space in between,

The "Me" that is watching and the "Thing" that is seen.

For if these were my thoughts, if these were my own,

I'd be the singer, not the one hearing the tone.

I am the sky; the thoughts are just the birds.

I am the page; the thoughts are just the words.

So let the stranger mutter, let the intruder shout,

Let them pace the hallways of my worry and my doubt.

They can inhabit the space, they can borrow the air,

But they are just a ghost, and I am the one who is there.

BUT MAYBE...

thoughts are not commands or facts,
just passing trains on shifting tracks.
They come, they go, they rise, they fall—

I do not have to board them all.
So I will watch and let it be,
no need to solve or disagree.

A breath, a pause, I let it pass,
like wind that moves through open glass.
And even when they shout out loud,

I am not lost within the crowd.
For I am more than what I think—
I choose the space between each blink

Psychosis

Reality—reality—what is it—what is it now?

It moves when I see it, it breaks when I doubt.

It hums in my teeth, it crawls in my head,

it says I'm awake—why does it feel like I'm dead?

The walls keep a count—yes, they count when I breathe,

they shift when I turn, they adjust underneath.

I stop—they go still—I move—they align,

like something is learning the shape of my mind.

The air isn't empty—it presses, it knows,

it tightens around every thought as it grows.

I think something once—and it's already there,

waiting ahead like it knew I'd get here.

A glance is a code—is it?—yes, it must be,

a blink is a signal directed at me.

I've seen this before—I have—I have—

or maybe I'm stuck in the moment I had.

My thoughts—my thoughts—stop—listen—

they don't feel like mine when I really listen.

They land fully formed, too sharp to deny,
like answers that came before questions could try.
Who put them there—who—who—who—
why do they fit like they already knew?
I try to pull back but I'm already through,
like thinking is something I'm no longer doing.
It's doing me.
It's using me—yes—
to map something out I can't fully address.
Each pattern connects to a deeper design,
like something is writing itself through my mind.
Is it mine—is it mine—or was it assigned?
Was I always this close to just losing my mind?
It fits—it fits—it fits too well—
like a truth I was never supposed to tell.
Time folds—time holds—time loops in my chest,
it won't let a second just come and then rest.
It stacks and it stacks and it stacks and it stacks
till I'm buried in moments that won't give me back.
The mirror—no—wait—don't—no—
it knows something I don't know.

That face—too late—out of place—

why is it moving before my face?

It's not behind—no—it's ahead—

it's where I'm going, not where I've been led.

It waits in the glass for me to align,

to step into it and leave this behind.

There's nothing beneath—no behind—no inside—

just layers collapsing that won't let me divide.

I reach for myself and there's nothing to find,

just echoes that answer before I decide.

And something is closing—yes—closing me in,

not outside the walls but beneath my own skin.

It tightens each thought till it sharpens to one—

and erases the rest like they never begun.

This is it—this is it—don't say it again—

if I name it once more it will know where I am.

I can't find the edge—I can't break the design—

just this thing

wearing my shape is

saying my name

like it's me.

BUT MAYBE...

I am here, though thoughts may bend,
and there are ways to help me mend.
A steady voice, a trusted guide,

can help me see the other side.
So I will reach, not face alone
the shifting ground I've always known.

Let others help me find what's true,
a clearer path to walk me through.
And though the storm may blur my view,

there's still a self that's steady, too.

Schizophrenia

The wallpaper breathes, it inhales all the light,

The static screams out in the dead of the night.

A thousand glass eyes staring out from the sink,

They know what I'm hiding, they know what I think.

The radio whispers my name through the teeth,

Of the secrets that burrow and fester beneath.

The unseen transmitters are trapped in my spine,

And the thoughts in my head are no longer just mine.

A symphony played on a violin string,

But the bow is a razor, and the choir won't sing—

They shriek and they argue, they beg me to run,

As the shadows grow teeth and eclipse the cold sun.

The mirror is lying, that face isn't me,

It's a hollowed-out shell where a mind used to be.

The gravity fails, and I'm falling upward,

Every sentence is broken, every logic absurd.

The floorboards are ticking, a countdown to zero,

In a story that features no savior or hero.

Just a labyrinth built out of panic and dread,

And the endless, loud riot inside of my head.

No anchor, no tether, just slipping through space,

While phantoms with my voice inhabit this place.

It's a prison of bone where the walls are designed,

To trap the last fragments of a shattering mind

BUT MAYBE…

I am here, though storms may start,
there's steady ground within my heart.
With help, with care, with voices true,

I can find what's real to hold onto.
So I will reach, I won't withdraw,
let trusted hands help what I saw.

Through shared reality, step by step,
I find the path where I'm best kept.
And though the noise may come and go,

there's strength in me I come to know.

Ekbom Syndrome

There’s a silver thread winding beneath the pale sheet,
A scuttle of ghosts and a drumbeat of feet.
It isn't a muscle, a twitch, or a nerve,
But a serpentine path with a sickening curve.
Beneath the forearm, where the blue veins run deep,
The tenants are waking while I try to sleep.
A knot in the shoulder, a slide through the wrist,
A phantom-like rope with a cold, wet-ink twist.
I reach for the surface to brush them away,
But they dive in the marrow and choose to stay.
The skin is a window, a thin, fragile glass,
Watching the shadows of "something" that pass.
It’s a ripple of motion, a shivering track,
With no way to follow and no turning back.
A secret migration, a silent command,
Moving like mercury under the hand.
The pulse is a rhythm they’ve learned to mimic,
A slow-motion riot, a visceral gimmick.

I've scoured the surface with water and lye,

To silence the movement, to give it the lie.

But the labyrinth's deep and the tunnels are old,

And the warmth of my blood keeps the parasites bold.

They weave through the tendon, they dance on the bone,

In a map of the body that's strictly my own.

It is logic defeated, it's reason undone,

A battle with shadows that cannot be won.

For the mind is a mirror that's fractured and wide,

And there is no place for the spirit to hide

When the hunter and hunted are sharing the skin,

And the call of the scuttle is coming from in.

BUT MAYBE…

feelings strong don't make them true,
the body speaks in signals, too.
Nerves can whisper, thoughts can grow,

and trick the senses what to know.
So I will pause before I chase
each fleeting sign I can't quite place.

A breath, a touch, a steady ground—
reminding me I'm safe and sound.
And if the feeling lingers near,

I'll meet it soft, not ruled by fear.
For I am more than what I feel—
and not all things I sense are re

Even the most fractured thoughts still come from a mind searching for meaning.

Part III: Memory & Identity

Alzheimer's

In the quiet drift of a thinning mind,
where names fall loose and won't rewind,
the days unspool like fragile lace,
each memory losing time and place.
A photograph with faceless smiles,
a voice once known now lost in miles,
the mirror holds a stranger's stare—
"Have we met?" it seems to ask there.
Keys in the fridge, a clock that lies,
a thousand small, unspoken goodbyes,
the past once bright now dim and far,
like reaching hands that miss their star.

BUT MAYBE…

beneath the fractured, fading light,

a spark endures beyond the night,

in touch, in tone, in soft refrain,

love hums where thought cannot remain.

Though words may slip and stories fall,

the heart remembers after all.

Amnesia

Amnesia is the fall of every name,

a life erased without a trace or flame.

No childhood songs, no whispered lullabies,

just empty echoes where the memory lies.

No “once upon,” no stories to retell,

no heaven saved, no past, no hint of hell.

A vacant page where chapters used to be,

a locked-out soul with no remembered key.

You face the mirror—someone stares you down,

a borrowed face, a lost, forgotten crown.

Your eyes search hard for something they once knew,

but even they can’t recognize it’s you.

Hands that once held love now drift in air,

they know the shape of touch—but no one’s there.

A phantom ache you cannot understand,

like reaching out with an unknowing hand.

They speak of you like someone still alive,

they say your past is something you survived.

They show you proof—your laughter, your embrace,

but all you see's a stranger in your place.

No roots below, no branches overhead,

just hollow ground where all your life has fled.

No sense of loss, no memory to grieve,

just something gone you cannot quite believe.

And in the quiet, cold and undefined,

there's not a single footprint in your mind.

No trace of who you were or where you've been—

just endless blank… where everything had been

BUT MAYBE…

I'll speak the nouns until they start to stick—
Coffee. Window. Cedar. Brick.
A rhythmic pulse to ground the drifting mind,

Leaving breadcrumbs for the self to find.
We'll look at the photos of people you knew,
Tracing the jawlines that look just like you.

I won't demand you remember the day,
I'll just tell the story till the fog thins away.
When the panic rises like a sudden tide,

Because the "Before" has nowhere to hide,
I'll be the anchor in the shifting sand—
A familiar voice, a steady hand.

Dissociative identity disorder

There's more than one of me in here—
not echoes, not illusions, not fear,
but shifting tides behind my eyes,
a crowded sky of different skies.
One wakes with fire in their chest,
one folds their hands and begs for rest,
one laughs too loud at nothing said,
one whispers, "Stay inside instead."
We argue over simple things—
what truth is, what tomorrow brings,
which mask to wear, which name to claim,
who gets the body, who takes the blame.
A mirror never quite agrees,
it flickers like a restless sea,
each glance reveals a different face
trying hard to take its place.
Sometimes we blend, a fragile thread,
a single voice from many heads,

sometimes we fracture, sharp and fast—
a present self that cannot last.
But listen close—beneath the noise,
the chaos, doubt, the broken poise,
there's not just madness in the storm—
there's every version trying to form.
Not lost—just many, undefined,
a constellation, not one mind.

BUT MAYBE...

I do not need to fight or hide,
these parts of me that live inside.
With gentle time, I start to see

they all have formed to shelter me.
So I will listen, slow and kind,
make room for all within my mind.

Build trust where once there may be fear,
and let each voice feel safe and heard here.
And piece by piece, not forced or fast,

I'll find a steadier ground at last.
Not broken parts I must deny—
but many selves learning to align.

Dissociating

I slip away without a sound,
though everything stays still around.
The walls, the light, the quiet air—
remain the same, but I'm not there.
My hands feel distant, far from me,
like borrowed parts I barely see.
They move, but slow, like delayed waves,
responding late to thoughts I gave.
The world turns soft along the seams,
like I am walking through a dream.
Voices echo, faint and thin,
as if they're locked outside my skin.
I nod and smile, I play along,
pretending nothing here is wrong.
An actor lost between the scene,
unsure of what is real or seen.
The mirror shows a face I know,
but feels like someone else's show.

I study eyes that should be mine,
yet feel detached, misaligned.
Time stretches out, then disappears,
I lose whole hours, days, or years.
It bends and breaks, then slips away,
no solid thread to hold the day.
Inside there's not a storm or fight,
just empty space, a hollowed quiet.
Not pain, not peace—just something gone,
a fading echo lingering on.
I reach for something real to hold,
a memory, a warmth, a soul—
but everything just slips right through,
like morning light or drops of dew.
Still deep beneath the distant air,
a quiet voice is waiting there:
"I'm still alive, though hard to see—
somewhere lost inside of me."

BUT MAYBE...

even here, I'm not gone through,
there are small ways to come back to.
A breath drawn slow, a hand, a name,

a steady pulse I can reclaim.
I'll name the room, the light, the air,
feel something solid, something there.

A textured thread, a sound, a sight—
small anchors pulling me to light.
And if I drift, I won't despair,

this mind has learned to take me there.
But I can guide it, soft and slow,
back to the self I come to know.

Mutism

My voice is tucked behind my chest,
a fragile thing that will not rest.
It stirs and waits, but won't break through,
no matter how I want it to.
The words arrive, then drift away,
like birds that fear too long a stay.
They circle close, then disappear,
as if my mouth is locked by fear.
They think my silence means there's none—
no thoughts, no feelings left undone.
But it is loud beneath my skin,
a storm of everything within.
I speak with ease inside my mind,
where every sentence flows aligned.
Where I am strong, where I am clear,
where no one sees the weight of fear.
But out aloud, the air feels tight,
like sound itself refuses flight.

My voice, a weight I cannot raise,

gets lost inside a silent haze.

So I will nod, and I will write,

and shrink into the quiet night.

But still inside, my truth will stay—

I am here, though words won't play

BUT MAYBE...

silence is not empty space,
it's just another way I pace.
My voice exists, though soft or slow,

it finds its path in time to flow.
So I will start in ways I can—
a written word, a gentle plan.

A nod, a sign, a steady breath,
small bridges built from quiet depth.
And I am more than what I say,

my worth does not depend on "okay."
For even silent, I am heard—
a whole, unspoken, living word.

Psychogenic non-epileptic seizures

It doesn't feel like "too much to feel,"

like something small, like something you heal,

it isn't soft, it isn't light—

it builds like pressure late at night.

A tightening deep within your chest,

a restless pulse that won't let rest,

a quiet warning, sharp and low,

a sense that something's wrong below.

You tell yourself, just let it pass,

like every storm you've known at last,

but this one grows, it doesn't fade,

it sharpens into something grave.

Your breathing slips, your heartbeat trips,

the world goes loose beneath your grip,

your senses blur, your thoughts delay,

like you are slowly pulled away.

Your fingers twitch, your muscles strain,

emotion turning into pain,

your body tenses, starts to shake,
a silent system bound to break.
And then you fall beyond your will,
your mind goes loud, your body still—
then not so still, it jerks, it bends,
like something inside you won't end.
You're there, you know, you almost see,
but not quite in your body, free,
you try to speak, to call, to stay,
but every word just slips away.
Too much to hold, too much to name,
too much that doesn't look the same,
a flood of something deep and true,
that breaks the bounds inside of you.
Your body speaks what you can't say,
it lets it out in its own way,
through shaking limbs and tightening breath,
a dance that feels too close to death.
And when it fades, you're left in place,
a hollow calm, a fragile space,
your body heavy, spirit worn,

like something in you has been torn.

You lie there quiet, scared to feel,

unsure of what your mind can heal,

as if one thought, one rise, one wave

could pull you back to what you gave.

But this is not some chosen act,

not something you can just hold back,

it's feeling vast, too deep, too true—

a storm your body lived through

BUT MAYBE…

I will ground when signs begin,
feel breath move slow beneath my skin.
Find something steady, safe, and near,

a voice, a touch, a place that's clear.
And after, I will treat with care
the weight my body chose to bear.

For healing grows when I can see—
this is not all of who I'll be.

When memory fades, identity does not disappear, it only becomes harder to recognize.

PART IV:
INNER BATTLES

Depression

The sky in my chest is a gangrenous sore,
A fountain of pus on a bone-splintered floor.
It breeds in the fissures, it poisons the blood,
A parasitic monster that thrives in the mud.
My thoughts are black beetles that lay eggs in my mind,
They chew through the retina, they leave me so blind.
They've swallowed the palate, they've severed the tongue:
I am the wreckage—the rot in the lung.
My lungs are two pockets of fluid and bile,
A warm, wet decay where I haven't been "me" for a while.
Each breath is a gurgle, a wet, snapping sound,
A bubbling confession of what's finally been found.
And time—just a carcass I wear like a shroud,
The silence is screaming. The silence is loud.
I spill from its gullet, a black, oily bile,
The harvest of maggots that's slept for a while.
I am the cancer. I am the death

BUT MAYBE...

even now, though faint and small,
a spark remains beneath it all.
Not loud, not bright, not burning fast—

just something steady that can last.
So I will rise in smaller ways,
not chase the sun, just face the day.

A breath, a step, a moment through—
that is enough to carry me, too.
And if I fall back into gray,

I'll trust it will not always stay.
For even night, no matter how long,
still turns, still breaks, still brings the dawn.

Intermittent Explosive Disorder

It builds in quiet, tight and low,
a pressure only I can know,
a spark beneath the surface line,
a fault that shifts without a sign.
A word, a look, a minor thing—
and suddenly my nerves all sting,
the air grows sharp, my chest feels caged,
something inside me turns to rage.
It rises fast, I lose the thread,
my thoughts outpace what's being said,
my voice, my hands, my heartbeat race—
I'm gone before I leave this place.
The moment cracks—I'm all flame,
no pause to question, think, or name,
just heat that floods and takes control,
a fire that overruns my soul.
And then it's done—as quick it came,
just silence, ash, and cooling shame,

the echoes of what I let through,

the things I said, the things I threw.

I stand inside the aftermath,

a stranger to my sudden wrath,

and try to gather what remains

of broken words and fractured names.

"I didn't mean it"—thin and late,

no match for what I let inflate,

a storm that left without a trace

except the ruin in its place.

But underneath the burst and blaze

are tangled fears and quieter waves,

a system wired to overflow,

a depth I'm only starting to know

BUT MAYBE…

I am not this flash of flame,
not every surge defines my name.
The heat may rise, the pulse may race,

but I can learn to slow its pace.
So I will watch for early signs—
tightened jaw, those warning lines.

Step back, breathe deep, give space, delay,
let seconds help it pass away.
And if I slip, I will repair,

with honest words and mindful care.
For strength is not in never breaking—
it's in the pause, the choice I'm making.

Bipolar

I rise too fast, I burn too bright,
I skip the night, refuse to rest,
my racing heart outpounds the dark,
a frantic drum inside my chest.
My thoughts ignite and multiply,
they crash, they spark, they amplify,
a thousand voices speak at once—
I chase them all, I don't ask why.
I laugh too loud, I feel too tall,
convinced I cannot break or fall,
I stretch beyond what I can hold,
and swear I do not need sleep at all.
I run on nothing, call it fuel,
I break each boundary, bend each rule,
I crown myself with fleeting fire
and play the king, the god, the fool.
Because it turns—
it always turns—

The glow collapses into gray,
the light retreats, it slips away,
the fire that once consumed the sky
now leaves me cold where embers lay.
I fall too far, I sink too deep,
I lose the strength to move or speak,
the mind that would not yield to night
now drowns inside a hollow sleep.
The bed's a weight, the air is stone,
I feel abandoned, cut, alone,
the voice that once was loud with pride
now tears apart my fragile bone.
Each second drags, each moment aches,
I feel the fault in all I make,
I count the breaths I barely take,
unsure how much more I can take.
I hate the climb, I hate the fall,
the brutal swing that steals it all,
no steady ground, no middle place—
just rising flame and shattered fall.
And still I stand between the strain,

between the loss, between the gain,

a fragile thread pulled tight and thin,

still holding through the storm and pain.

BUT MAYBE...

But I am not these shifting skies,
not only lows, not only highs.
I am the ground beneath it all,

the steady place that will not fall.
So when I rise, I'll breathe, take care,
move gently through the electric air.

And when I sink, I'll wait it through,
for tides will turn—as tides will do.
I'll build small anchors day by day,

soft routines to guide my way.
Not cured, not fixed, but learning still—
to ride the waves with strength and will.

ADHD

The sun goes down without my say,
the "To-Do" list rules the day.
I stand accused, my mind a maze,
defense a blur in sleepless haze.
My thoughts are tabs, all open wide,
three play music I cannot guide.
The one that screams I cannot find,
it hides, a shadow in my mind.
A firework trapped within a jar,
brilliant, chaotic, seeking far.
Its sparks press close against the glass,
a fleeting freedom that will not pass.
If only I could grasp the key,
to channel fire and set it free.
Yet here I whirl in endless tries,
a storm of focus behind my eyes.
Each fleeting thought ignites a flare,
a burst of brilliance caught in air.

I chase the sparks, they twist, they dart,

a restless tempest in my heart.

The world outside may move too slow,

but inside me, the currents flow.

Hyper-focus burns like molten steel,

a power I feel, a cage I feel.

And still I spin, both trapped and bright,

a firework blazing in the night.

If only I was strong enough,

and let the chaos fully free

If only I could turn the key,

and let the chaos fully free—

BUT MAYBE...

Perhaps the lock was never there,
just trembling hands and too much care.
What if the fire need not be tamed,

nor every spark be neatly named?
What if I breathe, and let it burn,
and trust the rhythm I can learn?

Not every thought must find its place,
not every race be won with grace.
I am the jar, the spark, the sky—

not just the storm that rushes by.
So I will stand, not chase, not flee,
and let the fire belong to me.

Autism

The light—stab—split—bright,

it burns, it blinds,

it steals my sight.

Too close, too sharp—

I cannot see,

shadows twist

and swallow me.

The hum coils,

it grinds, it bites,

It gnaws, it rages,

and fuels my fights.

Ribs rattle,

skull pounds,

it claws my core,

it shreds,

it spares no more.

Waves boom, crash, slam on me,

gasp, scream—

a storming sea.

Heat scorches skin,

sparks split the air,

pressure crushes bones,

panic everywhere.

Too much, too fast, too sharp, too tight,

the walls close in—

I choke in fright.

Brush, shift, sleeve, thread,

they shred, they tear,

they fill my head.

I can't—TOO LOUD—

don't make me stay,

the walls close in,

they shove, they sway.

No corner left, no shelter near,

it crushes, pounds,

it feeds my fear.

Thoughts twist, and spin— they overload,

They scream, they slam,

they crash, they implode.

Every strike—I reel, I fall,
another collides—
I feel it all.
Hands flail, shove, they try,
rock, shake, press, deny.
Flashing light, searing bright,
pricks and stabs,
it bites outright.
Buzzing shriek fills every space,
burning heat claws my face.
It breaks too wide—
I cannot reign,
too sharp, too bright,
too full of pain.
No power, no shield, no say,
it tears my mind
and burns away.
No end, no breath,
no place to hide,
I gasp, I thrash,
I'm torn inside.

It rages, presses,

will not cease,

my body crushed—

no hint of peace

BUT MAYBE…

To help it when it's tuned too loud,
a restless, shifting, pressing crowd,
I'll dim the glare, step from the noise,

and choose my calm, my space, my poise.
I am not wrong for how I feel,
for needing quiet, steady, real.

The way I move, the way I see,
is not a flaw—it's part of me.
My mind may map a different sky,

find patterns others pass right by.
Where hidden threads go left unread,
I walk the paths my thoughts have led.

So I will honor what I need,

take gentle time, move at my speed.

Not less, not broken, not to fix—

just made this way: complex, unique

OCD

The ceiling is a ledger of every sin I've thought,

A tally of the "Maybe" and the "What if" and the "Ought."

The Basal Ganglia is firing, a misfired, rusted spark,

Locking me in circles while I'm screaming in the dark.

It's the Error Signal screaming that the door is left unlatched,

Though my fingers feel the metal and the wood is bruised and scratched.

It's the Orbitofrontal ghost, the hyper-active glare,

Telling me the poison is in the water and the air.

I am scrubbing past the dermis, past the vanity of skin,

To reach the Amygdala where the terrors all begin.

It's a Glutamate explosion, a chemical cascade,

A biological betrayal that I never could evade.

The Compulsion is a coffin that I build with my own hands,

To satisfy a phantom that is issuing demands.

It's the Limbic System hijacking the logic of the mind,

Leaving every shred of "Reason" and "Safety" far behind.

BUT MAYBE…

thoughts are not commands or truth,
just echoes shaped by fear's uncouth.
The more I chase, the more they stay—

So I will learn a different way.
I'll let the question linger near,
without obeying every fear.

No rush to solve, no need to prove,
just let the wave pass through, then move.
And though it's hard, I'll still choose me,

not every thought deserves to be.
For strength is found, both calm and slow,
in letting go… and letting go.

Insomnia

I close my eyes, I beg, I plead,
but sleep won't give me what I need,
it lingers just beyond my reach,
a silent thing that will not teach.
I flip, I turn, I rearrange,
the dark feels thick, the air feels strange,
the minutes crawl, then race, then stall,
no sense of time at all, at all.
The clock glows red beside my bed,
it mocks the thoughts inside my head,
2:03… 2:04…
I swear I've lived this night before.
My mind won't dim, it sparks instead,
a storm of words I never said,
they echo sharp, they twist, they climb,
repeating lines a thousand times.
I try to count, I try to slow,
to let the heavy stillness grow,

but every breath just pulls me back
to restless thoughts I seem to lack.
The night drags on, too long, too steep,
I ache for just a thread of sleep,
but morning creeps without a sound—
and I have never once gone down.

BUT MAYBE...

rest is more than falling deep,
it's letting go, not forcing sleep.
A softened breath, a slower pace,

a gentle, unresisting space.
So I will lie and simply be,
no need to wrestle endlessly.

Even here, in wakeful night,
my body leans toward rest's soft light.
And sleep, in time, will find its way—

it always does, though it may stray.

Kufungisisa

My mind won't stop, it turns and spins,

a restless drum beneath my skin.

It circles back to where it's been,

and pulls me deeper in again.

The thoughts collect like heavy rain,

full of loss and quiet pain—

of what went wrong, of what might be,

of all that waits ahead for me.

They press against my chest so tight,

not fully fear, not quite a fright,

but something that won't fade away,

and lingers through both night and day.

Sleep arrives in tattered seams,

stitched together out of dreams.

But even there, I'm not set free—

the thoughts still follow endlessly.

The world moves on in light and sound,

in laughter rising all around,

but I am caught in one refrain,
replaying moments, looped in pain.
They call it thinking, soft and slow,
as if it's something I control.
But this is more than thoughts that pass—
it's being trapped in broken glass.
A river strong, it pulls me through,
with endless questions, none are new.
I fight to stand, I try to see,
but still it rushes over me.
And yet beneath the noise, the strain,
beyond the cycle of my brain,
there lies a quiet, steady breath—
a space untouched by thinking's depth.
I reach for it between each beat,
a fragile place where I can meet
the part of me that longs to rest—
and lay this storm inside my chest.

BUT MAYBE...

not each thought must be pursued,
not every fear deserves a mood.
The mind can wander, overplay—

that doesn't mean I have to stay.
So I will ground in what is now,
the breath I take, the here, the how.

A single moment, calm and true,
is something steady I can use.
And when my thoughts begin to race,

I'll meet them with a softer pace.
For peace is not in thinking through—
but in the space I give to you

Opposition defiance disorder

It's war in my chest from morning to night,
no pause, no surrender, just constant fight,
a battlefield drawn with each word that you say,
where I armor up fast and don't look away.
Every command is a line I must cross,
every demand feels like something I've lost,
so I stand in resistance, refuse to give in,
while the war drums are pounding loud under my skin.
It's clash after clash, no clear end in sight,
I'm both sides at once in this endless fight,
my mind like a storm that won't settle or sleep,
with trenches of anger that run dark and deep.
I brace for impact before it begins,
like I've learned every battle is something I'm in,
no safe ground to stand, no white flag to raise,
just fire in my chest and a permanent blaze.
And even in silence, the war doesn't cease,
there's no quiet moment, no treaty, no peace,

just echoes of conflict that endlessly roar—

a life lived inside of an unending war.

BUT MAYBE...

strength is not in every fight,
not every hill requires my might.
My voice is real, my will is strong—

but I can choose where I belong.
So I will pause before I react,
give space between the thought and act.

Ask, "Is this worth the fire I feel?"
and let that question help me heal.
I still have power, still have say—

in how I choose to move each day.
Not less, not weak, not giving in—
but learning where true strength begins.

Panic disorder

It starts as small, a subtle spark,
a sudden shift, a creeping dark,
a quiet hum beneath my skin
that builds a storm that pulls me in.
My chest locks tight, my breath goes thin,
my racing heart begins to spin,
it pounds so hard I swear it's wrong—
too fast, too wild, too loud, too strong.
The walls lean close, the floor won't stay,
the world tilts sharp and slips away,
my hands go cold, my vision blurs,
I lose what's mine, what's mine, what's hers.
I'm sure this time it's something real,
a break, a snap I cannot heal,
a hidden flaw, a final call—
this is the moment that I fall.
I try to breathe, count in and out,
but fear floods in and drowns my doubt,

it grips my ribs, it claws my chest,
it will not leave, it will not rest.
Then like a wave that breaks and dies,
it pulls away, it slowly dries,
the air returns, the pounding fades,
the terror loosens what it made.
No wound, no mark, no blood, no scar,
just proof of how relentless you are,
a war that strikes without a sound—
a false alarm that knocks me down.
And still I walk, still try to cope,
through quiet dread and fragile hope,
because I know how fast you start—
that sudden spark inside my heart

BUT MAYBE…

If i breathe, though breath feels small,
slow in, slow out—I'll ride it all.
Feet on the ground, I name what's true,

"I'm here, I'm safe, I'll make it through."
And when it passes, as it will,
I'll meet myself with kindness still.

For every wave I learn to ride
builds quiet strength I hold inside.

Phobias

The mind is a craftsman of velvet and steel,

Creating a prison that's hauntingly real.

It isn't a shadow or trick of the light,

But a pulse that goes screaming in middle of night.

Where logic is shattered and reason is thin,

The war is conducted from deep-down within.

Aphenphosmphobia: The skin is a border, a line in the sand,

Where fire erupts at the brush of a hand.

A hug is a shackle, a kiss is a sting,

The terror that human connection can bring.

To be held is to break, to be touched is to die,

Underneath the cold weight of a physical lie.

You walk through the world like a ghost in a shell,

In a private, untouched, and untouchable hell.

Cibophobia: How bitter the bread when the brain sees a blade,

Where every sweet morsel is subtly decayed.

The body is starving, the spirit is worn,

But the fruit on the vine feels like sulfur and thorn.

A fork is a needle, a glass is a trap,
A minefield laid out in a porcelain lap.
The fuel that we need is the foe that we fight,
In a battle for breath that lasts all through the night.
Decidophobia: A fork in the forest, a door in the hall,
And the fear that one gesture will ruin it all.
Is it left? Is it right? Is it "yes" or a "no"?
While the seeds of a thousand catastrophes grow.
The weight of the "maybe" is heavy as lead,
As a million "what-ifs" spin around in the head.
So you stand at the center, frozen and grey,
As the chance for a future slips slowly away.
Chronophobia: The clock is a hammer that beats on the bone,
A relentless and hollow and thundering tone.
Every second is stolen, a grain in the glass,
As the ghosts of the present all silently pass.
You can’t catch the minute, you can’t stop the day,
As the marrow of life is just washed clean away.
The heartbeat’s a countdown, the sun is a flare,
And the passing of time is a weight you can't bear.
Somniphobia: The eyelids grow heavy, the battle is near,

Where the softest of quiet is loudest with fear.

A physical panic, a violent revolt,

The nerves are struck dumb by a chemical bolt.

The heart screams a warning, a frantic alarm,

To save the whole self from an invisible harm.

To drift is to drown in an endless abyss,

And I cannot afford the dark comfort of this.

Panophobia: The fear has no face, yet it's always in sight,

A whisper that swells into deafening fright.

No corner is safe, no silence is still,

It bends every thought to its merciless will.

A breath is a burden, a step is a snare,

As danger takes shape in the thinnest of air.

The world is a storm with no eye and no end,

Where even your shadow's no longer a friend.

Yet—

deeper it digs, this velvet and steel,

Refining the cage to ensure it can't heal.

Each thought is conscripted, each feeling betrayed,

In a battlefield mind where no truce can be made.

The cracks are illusions, the light is a lie,

A tactic the psyche employs to comply.

For even resistance is bent to its scheme,

Rewritten and warped in the script of the dream.

No key waits in hand, no door left ajar,

Just echoes of who you once were, from afar.

And so the war rages, unending, concealed—

A mind turned against you that will not yield

BUT MAYBE…

fear can learn, and so can I,
to face it slow, not run or hide.
Not all at once, not forced or fast,

just steps so small they gently last.
A glance, a breath, a moment more,
a footstep closer than before.

Each time I stay, each time I see,
the fear loosens its hold on me.
And I am stronger than I feel,

even when the fear is real.
For courage isn't fear's defeat—
it's choosing still to stay and meet.

PTSD

It started with a lesson written deep into skin,
not spoken in words, but in where pain had been.
A rhythm of impact, a ritual of control,
each strike carving silence straight into my soul.
I learned how to read when the air turned to threat,
how danger could bloom before anything's set.
A glance held too long, a breath pulled too tight—
the moment before I disappeared from the light.
My body went quiet before it began,
already surrendering, already a plan:
don't fight it, don't cry, don't give it a sound,
because nothing in me was allowed to be found.
And afterward—nothing. Just ringing and breath,
that thin line of living that borders on death.
Bruises would blossom, then fade into lies,
while something much deeper refused to subside.
It never turned into a "then" I could leave,
just something that settled and learned how to breathe.

It walks in my chest, it sleeps in my spine,
it waits in the dark for a moment like mine.
It wakes without warning, it tears through the day,
in flashes and fragments that won't stay away.
It steals every second that almost feels still,
reminding my body it never had will.
There isn't a world I can prove that is real,
just shapes that I move through and nothing I feel.
A body I'm trapped in that doesn't believe
it's already gone and forgot how to leave.
My pulse turns against me, it pounds like a threat,
like something inside hasn't finished me yet.
My hands move on instinct—to cover, to brace,
like I'm still being hurt in a safer place.
And anything gentle feels wrong in my chest,
like kindness is something I have to reject.
I turn from the light like it's not meant for me,
like good things are traps I was trained not to see.
There is no release, no escape, no reward,
just time dragging on like a life I can't afford.
No healing, no ending, no point to restore

just something still breathing

that isn't me anymore.

BUT MAYBE...

I will breathe, slow, deep, and low,
remind my heart of what I know.
A name, a place, the day, the year—

I anchor gently back to here.
And step by step, I'll learn to see
the past is not controlling me.

For though it shaped the path I've known,
my life today is still my own.

Separation anxiety

I don't just miss you when you go—

I come undone in ways I know.

The moment that your hand leaves mine,

The world distorts, misdrawn, misaligned.

The colors run, the edges break,

My breath turns thin with every ache.

It feels like air is not my own,

Like I must earn each fragile loan.

It isn't space that makes me fear,

It's you becoming gone from here.

Not miles between, but you erased—

A life where I am not a place.

Each "goodbye" sounds too much like "end,"

Each silence twists what I defend.

A second passed becomes a sign

That something's wrong I can't define.

I try to reason, to be still,

To bend my thoughts back to my will.

"They're safe, they'll come, you'll be okay"—

But doubt corrodes what I can say.

My mind builds loss from fragile air,

Finds ghosts in things that aren't there.

It digs through "maybe," dark and deep,

And buries me in what-ifs steep.

Without you near, I start to shrink,

Fall inward faster than I think.

Like I am less, like I am small,

Like I might vanish most of all.

They say, "Be strong, stand on your own,"

But they've not felt this kind of alone.

Alone's a scream beneath the skin,

A pounding fear that lives within.

A child inside me begs and cries,

Afraid of all the "what ifs," "whys."

No one can hear, no one can see

The war that absence makes of me.

And when you come back—safe, in view,

I don't feel peace… not right away, true.

I feel the weight of what I knew:

How close I came to losing you—

And losing me in losing you.

BUT MAYBE…

love is not so quick to fade,
nor bonds so easily unmade.
What's real remains beyond the view,

even when they're not in front of you.
So I will breathe and gently stay,
let time and trust show me the way.

A part of them I carry near,
in memory, in love, in here.
And I am safe, though we're apart,

their presence lives within my heart.

Sleep paralysis

Pinned to the bed where the darkness creeps,

Half in a nightmare, half out of sleep.

Eyes open wide but my body won't move,

Trapped in a terror I didn't choose.

The air feels heavy, thick with dread,

A silent pressure upon my chest.

I try to scream, but nothing comes—

Just a hollow echo, a voiceless hum.

Something stands where the shadows bend,

Not quite a shape I comprehend.

It watches close, it knows I'm aware,

Breathing slow in the frozen air.

My fingers beg just to twitch or shake,

My lungs plead hard for one deep break.

But time is cruel in this in-between,

Where fear feels realer than any dream.

Then suddenly—like a snapped-off thread,

The weight is gone, the figure has fled.

I gasp for life, I move, I see…

But part of it stays, still clinging to me.

BUT MAYBE...

this will pass, it always does,
my body caught between because
of sleep and wake that overlap—

a moment in a drifting gap.
So I will breathe, though small and slow,
and trust this state will come and go.

I'll move a finger, toe, or hand,
and gently guide what feels unmanned.
And when it breaks, as it will do,

I'll ground myself in what is true.
For even fear that feels this near
cannot remain, cannot stay here.

Tourette syndrome

It starts as a hum where the bone meets the skin,
A tightening coil that is buried within.
It's the weight of a shadow, the pull of a moon,
A static-filled silence that's ending too soon.
It's a pressure that builds like a storm in the chest,
A frantic "not yet" that refuses to rest.
A prickle, a heat, or a localized spark,
Like a phantom finger that leaves its own mark.
It's the breath before diving, the tension of wire,
A physical thirst and a kinetic fire
To fight it is holding a gale in a jar,
While feeling the sting of a traveling star.
The more that you push, the more that it grows,
Until every fiber and ligament knows.
Then comes the snap—the release of the spring,
The jerk of the neck or the voice as it rings.
The muscle commands what the mind didn't plan,
A sudden upheaval of "won't" into "can."

It’s the body’s own lightning, a jagged escape,

Giving the invisible pressure a shape.

A moment of stillness, a hollow reprieve,

As the tide pulls away from the shore of the sleeve.

The itch has been quieted, the debt has been paid,

Until the next spark in the marrow is made.

It isn't a glitch, but a pulse all its own—

The wild, restless music of synapse and bone.

BUT MAYBE...

I am not these tics alone,
they're just one part of what I've grown.
My mind, my heart, my voice, my view

are bigger than what tics can do.
So I will stand without disguise,
no need to shrink, no need to hide.

Let others learn, let kindness lead,
and give myself the space I need.
For I am whole in all I show—

and worthy, just the way I go.

Emotional regulation disorder

It starts so small—a fragile spark,

a sudden shift, a subtle mark.

A word that lands a little too deep,

and pulls me under without a leap.

I do not walk where feelings go,

I'm dragged beneath their undertow.

A silent force I cannot see

still finds its way to swallow me.

A glance becomes a sharp goodbye,

a quiet room a reason why.

And I am every hurt I've known,

each aching age at once full-grown.

My chest is tight with too much flame,

no space inside to hold the same.

Love twists to fear in just one breath,

each joy feels balanced close to death.

I try to speak, but lose control,

my voice too loud, too much, too full.

Or else it fades and leaves me there,

drowning softly in open air.

And when the storm has passed me through,

regret arrives in heavy hue.

I trace the words I can't erase,

and feel the shame I cannot face.

I play it back, each moment clear,

each sound, each glance, each thread of fear.

I wish that I could softer be,

more calm, more safe, more easy—free.

BUT MAYBE…

But this is not a path I chose,
it's how my restless body flows.
A heart that never learned to slow,

a mind that feels too much, too so.
And still beneath the crashing tide,
a quiet hope I try to hide—

that one day I might stand and say:
these waves won't take my breath away.

Some of the hardest battles are the ones no one else can see, but they are still battles worth surviving.

PART V:
SELF & PERCEPTION

Body dysmorphia disorder

The mirror bends before I do,
it tells me things that can't be true,
it sharpens flaws no one else sees,
then brings me slowly to my knees.
I trace my face like it's a map,
each line, each curve—a kind of trap,
a thousand versions in my mind,
none of them are ever kind.
I tilt my head, adjust the light,
convince myself I'm seeing right,
but every angle shifts the lie—
I look again, I don't know why.
The world says, "you look just the same,"
but sameness doesn't stop the shame,
their words fall off, they never stick,
the doubt is louder, sharp and quick.
My thoughts enlarge the smallest part,
turn passing glances into art,

a gallery of silent critique,
where every feature feels too weak.
I measure worth in fractured sight,
compare myself from day to night,
and lose the shape of who I am
inside a lens that always scams.
But somewhere past the glass and glare,
a quieter truth is waiting there,
unchanged by angles, light, or view—
a self that isn't split in two.
It doesn't shift with every glance,
or hinge on some imagined chance,
it isn't built from what I see
reflected back accusing me.
And though the mirror pulls me near,
and fills my chest with doubt and fear,
I am not what it distorts—
not all these harsh, relentless thoughts.
So maybe I can learn to stand
without obeying its command,
to look, then slowly look away,

and let those lies not have their say.

And even if I still believe

the worst of what I think I see,

there's more to me than warped reflection—

I am not just misperception

BUT MAYBE...

I must remember to practice softer sight,
not every thought deserves the fight.
I am not sums of "fix" or "flaw,"

but more than what the mirror saw.
And step by step, I'll learn to see
a kinder truth reflected back at me.

Avoidant personality disorder

You learn, with time, to disappear—
not gone, but faint, not fully here,
like whispered breath on glass so thin
that fades before it settles in.
A crowded room feels loud and bright,
each glance a test, each word a fight,
you hold your voice, you play it small,
afraid to speak, afraid to fall.
You practice lines you'll never say,
you shape each word, then turn away,
you smooth the edges, make them right,
then keep them hidden out of sight.
Because it's safer not to try
than risk the chance of wondering why—
why you weren't enough to stay,
why they might slowly turn away.
You ache to reach, to be let through,
to let someone get close to you,

but every step feels far too steep,
like waking something best asleep.
What if they see what you can't hide?
Or worse—just look, then step aside?
What if you give your truest part
and they decide you're not worth heart?
So you retreat before the fall,
build quiet walls, avoid it all,
convince yourself you're better alone
than risking being overthrown.
You read too much in every pause,
create rejection without cause,
a silence grows, your thoughts take flight,
and turn the small things into slight.
You make yourself a safer frame,
less to reject, less space for blame,
become a version trimmed and mild—
acceptable, but not your child.
And still beneath the fear you keep

a longing buried far too deep,

a quiet hope you can’t undo—

to still be seen,

and still be you

BUT MAYBE...

So I will start with steps so slight,
a word, a glance, a brief invite.
Not leaps, but inches, soft and slow—

still forward counts, and that I know.
I may feel fear, my voice may shake,
but courage grows with steps I take.

I'm more than doubt, more than retreat—
there's strength each time I choose to meet.
And if I stumble, turn, or hide,

I'll meet myself with gentler eyes.
For every step I dare to try
is proof I'm stronger than "goodbye

Antisocial Personality Disorder

I learned that faces are puzzles to crack,
no conscience to guide me, no feeling to lack.
A smile is a weapon, a tear is a tool,
the world is a board and I play it like cruel.
They whisper "you're hollow, there's nothing inside,"
like something once sacred curled up and then died.
But I am not empty—I'm sharpened, aware,
a blade in the silence, a cut in the air.
Your fear is a rhythm, a pulse I can chase,
it pounds like a drum that I never embrace.
I hear it, I use it, I bend it to will,
a storm passing through me, but I remain still.
Remorse is a ghost that won't answer my call,
I mimic its shadow, I counterfeit all.
I shape it in language, I counterfeit pain,
but nothing takes root—just a permanent stain.
And still in the dark, when the noise disappears,
no echoes of guilt and no trace of your tears,

I pause for a second—just one fractured view:

what's it like to break… and be broken too?

BUT MAYBE...

You don't need to weep to be part of the fold,
Or force a new shape into someone else's mold.
But there is a strength in the hands that don't tear,

A dignity found in a life that is fair.
I'll be the anchor when the impulse is loud,
The one steady face in the shifting crowd.

Not to "fix" what is wired in the marrow and bone,
But to ensure that you don't have to navigate alone.
We'll trade the wildfire for a controlled, steady spark,

And map out the traps that wait in the dark.
Control is a weapon, but structure is key;
Let's build a version of you that is free.

Apotemnophilia

There's a line my mind has drawn
where my body carries on,
past the place that feels like me—
past a quiet boundary.
It follows me through every day,
a ghost I cannot look away.
In every step, in how I stand,
I feel too much of what I am.
They see a whole, completed frame,
they call it healthy, call it sane.
But I feel excess, sharp and loud,
like wearing skin that's not allowed.
I try to reason, try to fight,
convince myself that this is right—
that I am fine just as I stand,
no need to redraw what's been planned.
But still the thought returns again,
persistent as a silent friend:

What if less could make me whole?
What if absence fits my soul?
It's not a wish born out of pain,
not something wild or to entertain.
It's steady, quiet, deeply known—
a truth that feels like it's my own.
And yet I stand, divided here,
between what's felt and what they fear.
A body seen, a self-unsure,
of what it means to feel secure.
So I exist in in-between,
in what is shown and what is seen—
holding a line I can't erase,
searching for a fitting place.

BUT MAYBE...

It's a dissonance deep in the marrow and bone,
A feeling of carrying a weight not your own.
We'll honor the struggle, the strange, silent ache,

Without rushing a choice that the body can't take.
When the urge is a tide that pulls at the shore,
And the skin that you're in feels like a locked door,

We'll focus on breath, on the pulse, on the heat—
On keeping the "now" beneath both of your feet.

Excoriation disorder

My fingers know the places best—
the slightest rise, the smallest crest,
they scan my skin like searching light
for something rough to make it right.
A bump, a flake, a jagged seam,
becomes the center of the scene,
I lean in close, I start to fix,
get lost inside the tiny risks.
I pick at edges, peel them back,
convince myself it's what I lack—
if I can smooth this one small part,
I might feel quiet in my heart.
But minutes stretch and drift away,
my hands don't listen when I say,
"enough, just stop"—the words fall thin,
the urge has already settled in.
The sting arrives, a fleeting burn,
a lesson I refuse to learn,

yet still I chase that moment's peace
that never comes, that will not cease.
I trace again what I just made,
new broken ground where skin once stayed,
a cycle drawn in careful lines,
repeating shapes, familiar signs.
And when I stop, I finally see
the cost of what it took from me—
the marks, the red, the quiet shame,
the way it always feels the same.
But even here, with trembling hands,
there's something small that understands:
this isn't failure carved in skin,
it's something deeper pulling in.
A need to smooth, to calm, control,
to quiet something in my soul—
and though it shows in what I do,
it isn't all of what is true.

BUT MAYBE…

So maybe next time, just a breath,
a second's pause to interrupt,
not perfect, no—not all at once,

just one small moment of "don't touch."
And if I can't—if I give in,
and trace again along my skin,

I'll try to leave a little grace
for every mark I can't erase.

Narcissistic personality disorder

I speak like I'm certain, like I own every room,

But inside there's a quiet I'm afraid to consume.

I polish my stories till they glitter and shine,

So no one can question what I fear isn't mine.

If I sound like I'm bigger, it's not pride that you hear,

It's the echo of doubt that I'm drowning in here.

I reach for your praise like it's air I must breathe,

Every glance that you give is a reason to be.

When your focus drifts off, I feel edges unwind,

Like I'm losing the shape that was holding my mind.

So I pull you back close, maybe more than I should,

Trying hard to feel real in the only way I could.

I know it's too much—every word, every claim,

Every spark of attention that I turn to a flame.

But if I grow quiet, if I loosen my grip,

I'm afraid I might fade… I might suddenly slip.

So I build up a version that's steady and strong,

Even if deep down I know something's wrong.

I'm not chasing a crown or a spotlight to prove—

I'm just trying to hold onto something that's true

BUT MAYBE...

worth is not in being seen
as flawless, perfect, or pristine.
It lives within the honest view

of all I am—the strong and true.
So I will look a little deeper,
not just the image I am keeper.

I'll hear the voices not my own,
and let their truths help shape my tone.
To give, to feel, to truly see

the world beyond just centering me.
For strength is found, both brave and rare,
in choosing truth, in choosing care.

Paranoid Personality Disorder

They say the world is calm and still,
but I can hear its hidden will.
Each glance a clue, each word a test,
no place for ease, no space for rest.
A whispered laugh, a subtle stare—
I feel the meaning lurking there.
Your smile bends just slightly wrong,
like it's been practiced far too long.
I weigh each pause, I track each tone,
turn passing moments into stone.
A puzzle built from things unsaid,
where doubt and danger softly spread.
Trust is a door I cannot find,
it shifts and locks inside my mind.
Even your kindness feels rehearsed,
a careful script that masks the worst.
Nothing is neutral, all must lean—
a hidden motive in between.

I guard myself, I stand apart,
a fragile shield around my heart.
I want to think your hands are true,
that there's no harm concealed in you.
But hope's a risk I can't defend—
it leaves me open in the end.
So I stay watchful, eyes aware,
of every silence in the air.
Alone, though voices fill the room,
I brace myself for coming doom.

BUT MAYBE...

not all shadows signal threat,
not every fear is danger met.
A thought can feel both sharp and right,

yet still be shaped by inner fright.
So I will pause and gently weigh
what feels so certain in the day.

Seek steady proof, let others in,
allow small trust to now begin.
And though I guard what's close to me,

I don't need walls for all to see.
For strength can grow, both calm and wise,
in learning truth beyond disguise.

Dyslexia

The letters lean and turn around,
They flip themselves without a sound.
A “b” becomes a “d” in flight,
The day can feel reversed from night.
The lines don’t stay where they belong,
They twist and pull the words along.
I start to read from left to right,
Then lose the path mid-sentence sight.
It’s like the world’s a mirror glass,
Where forwards shifts as moments pass.
Each word I knew, so clear before,
Comes back reversed, and something more.
A “was” might turn itself to “saw,”
A simple rule forgets its law.
The start and end refuse their place,
They trade their steps, they switch their face.
I trace the page, then trace again,
The ink won’t settle in my brain.

It slips like water through my hand,
A language hard to understand.
But in this maze of flipped design,
A different kind of truth is mine.
I see both sides, I trace what's through—
What's backwards there is forward, too.
For every word that turns away,
Another finds a different way.
And though the path may bend and skew,
My thoughts still shine in their own view.

BUT MAYBE...

My mind sees patterns, wide and bright,
in ways beyond the printed sight.
What takes me time is not a flaw—

just a different way I draw.
So I will read at my own pace,
give learning time and steady space.

Not less, not slow, not left behind—
just working with a different mind.
And every word I learn to see

is proof of strength inside of me.

The way you see yourself can shift, but it is never fixed beyond change.

PART VI: BELONGING & CHANGE

Culture shock

I packed my world in careful hands,
then crossed unfamiliar lands.
I brought my language, clothes, and name,
yet nothing here would feel the same.
The streets moved fast in different ways,
new sounds filled up my nights and days.
The words were sharp, the silence strange,
and every comfort seemed to change.
The food held flavors I'd not known,
each crowded room still felt alone.
I smiled when I did not understand,
and nodded more than I had planned.
I missed the songs my people knew,
the sky at home, its softer hue.
I missed the way my mother spoke,
the little laughs behind each joke.
Here even time felt pulled askew,
too fast, too slow, then strange and new.

BUT MAYBE...

I learned that homesickness can stay
and echo softly through each day.
But slowly, softly, things drew near—

a place, a face, a voice made clear.
The foreign roads grew less unknown,
and pieces formed a second home.

Now I still carry where I'm from,
its steady beat, a quiet drum.
But I have learned, through all I face,

to hold two worlds in one small space.

Belonging is not lost in change, it is rebuilt within it.

So,

If you saw yourself in these pages,

know this,

-you are not alone,

you are not broken,

and this is not the end of your story.

-Even in the quiet,

even in the dark,

something in you is still reaching forward.

And that... is enough.

"Pause & Reflect"

In the end, take a moment.

- **Which piece stayed with you the longest?**

- **What emotion did it bring up?**

- **Can you name one thing you're feeling right now?**

Now write one sentence to yourself, not perfect, just honest.

Made in the USA
Coppell, TX
27 June 2026

83165937R00098